Graf von Loeben and the Legend

Allen Wilson Porterfield

Graf von Loeben and the Legend

Table of Contents

Graf von Loeben and the Legend..1
   Allen Wilson Porterfield..1
   I...1
   II..6
   III...14
   FOOTNOTES:...18

Graf von Loeben and the Legend

Allen Wilson Porterfield

Kessinger Publishing reprints thousands of hard-to-find books!

Visit us at http://www.kessinger.net

- I
- II
- III
- FOOTNOTES:

Modern Philology

VOLUME XIII October 1915 NUMBER 6 (pp. 65-92)

ALLEN WILSON PORTERFIELD

GRAF VON LOEBEN AND THE LEGEND OF LORELEI

I

The devotees of Apollo have to give a good account of themselves in Olympia before, they can become *persona grata* on Olympus. They spend their lives, more or less, at the various games of poetry. Some, like Goethe, win in the majority of trials, and then we study all of their records regardless of their individual excellence. Some like Immermann in *Oberhof*, win only once, but this is sufficient to insure immortality. Some play and joust, run and wrestle with constancy and grace; their records, just after starting and just before finishing, are interesting, but in the end they are always defeated. And when this is the case, posterity, lay and initiated, forgets their names and concerns itself in no wise with their records, unless it be for statistical purposes. It is to the latter class that Graf von Loeben[1] belongs. For twenty-five years he was a perpetual, loyal, chivalric contestant in the Olympic vale of poetry. His running was interesting, but he never won; he never

Graf von Loeben and the Legend

wrote a single thing that everybody still reads for its own sake.

Aside from his connection with the Lorelei-matter, Graf von Loeben is, therefore, at present, a wholly obscure, indeed unknown, Poet. The large *Konversations-Lexikons*[2] of Meyer and Brockhaus say nothing about him, unless it be in the discussion of some other poet with whom he associated. Of the twenty best-known histories of German literature, some of which treat nothing but the nineteenth century, only six contain his name, and these simply mention him either as a member of the Dresden group of pseudo-romanticists, or as one of those *Afterromantiker* who did yeoman service by way of bringing real romanticism into disrepute through their unsubstantial, imitative, and formless works. And this is true despite the fact that Loeben was an exceedingly prolific writer and a very popular and influential man in. his day. Concerning his personality, Muncker says: "Die Tiefe und WAerme seines leicht erregbaren GemUethes, seine Herzensreinheit, seine schwAermerische Hingabe an alles SchOene und Edle sowie sein zartes TactgefUehl erwarben ihm bei Freunden und Bekannten das Lob einer schOenen Seele in des Wortes schOenster Bedeutung."[3]

As to his poetic ability from the point of view of quantity, one can only marvel at the amount he produced in the time at his disposal; his creative works cover all types and sorts of literature.[4] He is best known for his numerous poems and his *magnus opus*, *Guido*, a novel of 360 pages, written under the pen-name of "Isidorus Orientalis," and intended as a continuation of Novalis' *Ofterdingen* ; he used Tieck's notes for this purpose. He wrote also a great number of letters, between 60 and 70 elaborate reviews, and some critical essays, the best of which seems to be his commentary to Madame de Stael's *De l'Allemagne*, while he translated from Anacreon, Dante, Guarini, Horace, Ovid, Petrarch, Vergil, and others, and left a number of fragments including the outline of a pretentious novel of which Heinrich von Veldeke, whom he looked upon as "der Heilige des Enthusiasmus," was to be the hero. And he was, incidentally, an omnivorous reader, for, as he naively said:

Viele BUecher muss ich kennen,
Denn die Menschen kenn' ich gern.[5]

As to his originality, another confession is significant:

Graf von Loeben and the Legend

Ja, es gibt nur wenig Leute,
Deren SchUeler ich nicht bin.[6]

No attempt, however, has as yet been made at even an eclectic edition of his numerous finished works, a few of which are still unpublished, many of which are now rare.[7]

As to his standing with his literary contemporaries, Eichendorff admitted[8] that Loeben influenced him as a man and as a poet; it was he who induced Eichendorff to write some of his earlier works under the pen-name of "Florens." And Eichendorff in turn credited Goethe with the remark[9] that "Loeben war der vorzUeglichste Dichter jener Zeit." His influence on Platen[10] is not quite so certain; Loeben was Platen's senior by ten years, and they resembled each other in their ability to employ difficult verse and strophe forms, and Platen read Loeben in 1824. Kleist interested himself in Loeben sufficiently to publish one of his short stories in his *AbendblAetter*, but only after he had so thoroughly revised it that Reinhold Steig says: "Ich wUerde als Herausgeber die ErzAehlung sogar unter Kleists *Parerga* aufnehmen."[11] His connection with, and influence upon, the Dresden group of romanticists, including Tieck, is a matter of record,[12] and Fouque looked upon him as a poet of uncommon ability.[13]

But let no one on this account believe that Loeben was a great poet and that the silence concerning him is therefore grimly unjust. Goethe, whether he made the foregoing remark or not, at least received[14] Loeben kindly; but he received others in the same way who were not poets at all. Eichendorff said: "Loeben. Wunderbar poetische Natur in stiller VerklAerung."[15] But Eichendorff was then only nineteen years old, and he later took this back. Herder was moved to tears[16] on reading Loeben's *Maria*, but Herder was easily moved, and he died soon after; he would in all probability have changed his mind too. Friedrich Schlegel, on the other hand, was not justified in calling[17] the pastoral poems in *Arkadien* "Schafpoesie." Uhland praised[18] these same poems; but he reminded Loeben in no uncertain terms, that the chief characteristic of southern poetry was "Phantasie," while that of the northern poets was "GemUeth," and that the attempt to revive the spirit of Guarini, Cervantes, and their kind was not well taken.

That Loeben has been so totally neglected by historians and encyclopedists is simply a case of that disproportion that so frequently characterizes general treatises. Loeben is entitled to some space in large works on German literature; but he was, like many another who has been given space, a weak poet. And the sort of weakness, with which he was endowed can be brought out by a discussion of two of his novelettes, *Das weisse Ross*,[19] and *Leda,* neither of which is by any means his best work, and neither of which seems to be his worst. But, to judge from what has been said of his prose works in general, both are quite typical.

The plot so far as the action[20] is concerned is as follows: Otto owes the victory he won at a tournament in NUernberg largely to the beauty and agility of his great white horse Bellerophon. Siegenot von der Aue had seen him and his horse perform and determined to obtain Bellerophon, if possible, for, owing to a curse pronounced on his family by a remote ancestor, Siegenot must either win at the next tournament or become a monk, which he does not wish to do. Both he and Otto love Felicitas, the niece of Graf Berthald. Siegenot secures Bellerophon, is victorious at the tournament, though seriously wounded, and is nursed back to health by Otto and Felicitas. It is Otto, however, who wins Felicitas through his chivalric treatment of his rival. The two are married, while Siegenot rides away on the great white horse Bellerophon.

It is such creations that make us turn away from Loeben. Alas for German romanticism if this story were wholly typical of it! It contains the traditional conceits of the orthodox romanticists, but applied in such a sweet, lovely, pretty fashion! One woman is placed between two men, for in that way Loeben could best bring out his philosophy of friendship. The only change, it seems, that he ever made in this arrangement was to place one man between two women. The sick-bed is poetized as the cradle of knowledge, for in it, or on it, we become introspective and learn life. Old chronicles, tournaments, jewelry, precious stones, Maryism, nature from every conceivable point of view, dreams and premonitions, visions and hallucinations, religion of the renunciatory type, the pain that clarifies, the friendship that weeps, Catholic painting and lute music, and love—human and divine—these are the main themes in this tale. Lyrics and episodic stories are interpolated, obsolete words and stylistic archaisms occur. In short, the novelette reads like an amalgamation of Novalis without his philosophy, Waekenroder without his suggestiveness, and Tieck without his constructive ability.

The story[21] entitled Leda is again typical of Loeben. Briefly stated, the plot is as follows: Leda, the daughter of a Roman duke, loves Cephalo, who is a gentleman but not a nobleman, and is loved by him. Her father, however, has forced her to become engaged to Alberto, a man of high degree, whom she does not love. The wedding is imminent, and Leda is sorely perplexed. Her father does not know why she is so indifferent to the approaching event and accordingly sends her to a distant and lonely castle in the hope that she may become interested, at least, in her own nuptials. While there she drowns herself in the swan lake. Alberto drops out of the story, and Cephalo becomes the intimate friend of the duke. Previous to this Alberto had ordered a certain painter to paint a picture of "Leda and the Swan." Danae, the daughter of an old, unscrupulous antiquarian, was seen by Cephalo while posing as a model for Leda. Enraged at this, she tells her father that she will not be appeased until married to Cephalo. But she loses her life through the falling of an old, dilapidated castle wherein she has been keeping an unconventional tryst, and Cephalo becomes the intimate friend of the painter.

Loeben's ideas and technique stand out in every line of this story. One woman is placed between two men, unexpected friendships are developed, the lute and the zither are played in the moonlight, love and longing abound, nature is made a confidant, *der Zaubern der Kunst* is overdone, familiar stories—Leda and the Swan, Actaeon and Danae—are interwoven, there are manifest reminiscences of *Emilia Galotti* and *Ofterdingen*, and the prose is uncommonly fluent. The only character in the entire narrative who has any virility is the antiquarian, and he is one of the meanest Loeben ever drew. Alberto has no will at all, Leda not much, Cephalo less than Leda, and Danae is without character. In short, the only valuable, part of the story lies in its approach to a development of the psychology of love in art. But it is only an approach; and it does not make one feel inclined to read a vast deal more of the prose works of Graf von Loeben.

As to Loeben's lyrics,[22] they are irregular, inconsistent, and odd as to orthography,[23] melodious and flowing in form, poor in ideas, rich in feeling that frequently sounds forced, representative of nearly all the important Germanic, Romance, and Oriental verse and strophe forms, reminiscent of his reading[24] in many instances, and romantic as a whole, especially in their constant portrayal of longing. Loeben was the poet of *Sehnsucht*. He tried always *das Nahe zu entfernen und das Ferne sich nahe zu bringen*. With a few conspicuous exceptions, his lyrics resemble those of Geibel somewhat in form and treatment. Poetry and individual poets receive grateful consideration, the seasons are overworked, love rarely fails and nature never, wine and the Rhine are not forgotten, and the South is poetized as the land of undying inspiration. Of their kind, and in their way, Loeben's poems are nearly perfect.[25] There are no expressions that repel, no verses that jar, no poems that wholly lack fancy, and there are occasional evidences of the inspiration that rebounds. It would be presumptuous to ask for a more amiable poem than "FrUehlingstrost" (46), or for a neater one than "Der NichterhOerte" (121), or for a more gently roguish one than the triolett[26] entitled "Frage" (55).

But be his poems never so good, there is no reason why Loeben should be revived for the general reader. His prose works lack artistic measure and objective plausibility; his lyrics lack clarity and virility; his creations in general lack the story-telling property that holds attention and the human-interest touches that move the soul. His thirty-nine years were too empty of real experience;[27] his works are not filled with the matter that endures. And it is for this reason that they ceased to live after their author had died. His connection with this earth was always just at the snapping-point. His works constitute, in many instances, a poetic rearrangement of what he had just latterly read. And when he is original he is vacuous. To emphasize his works for their own sake would consequently be to set up false values. Loeben can be studied with profit only by those people who believe that great poets can be better understood and appreciated by a study of the literary than by a study of the economic background. To know Loeben[28] throws light on some of his much greater contemporaries—Goethe, Eichendorff, Kleist, Novalis, Arnim, Brentano, Uhland, GOerres, Tieck, and possibly Heine.

II

But it is not so much the purpose of this paper to evaluate Loeben's creations as to locate him in the development of the Lorelei-legend, and to prove, or disprove, Heine's indebtedness to him in the case of his own poem of like name. The facts are these:

In 1801 Clemens Brentano published at Bremen the first volume of his _Godwi and in 1802 the second volume at the same place.[29] He had finished the novel early in 1799—he was then twenty-one years old. Wieland was instrumental in securing a publisher.[30] Near the close of the second volume, Violette sings the song beginning:

    Zu Bacharach am Rheine
    Wohnt eine Zauberin.

That this now well-known ballad of the Lorelei was invented by Brentano is proved, not so much by his own statement to that effect as by the fact that the erudite and diligent Grimm brothers, the friends of Brentano, did not include the Lorelei-legend in their collection of *579 Deutsche Sagen*, 1816. The name of his heroine Brentano took from the

Graf von Loeben and the Legend

famous echo-rock near St. Goar, with which locality he became thoroughly familiar during the years 1780–89. No romanticist knew the Rhine better or loved it more than Brentano. "Lore" means[31] a small, squinting elf; and is connected with the verb "lauern." The oldest form of the word is found in the *Codex Annales Fuldenses*, which goes back to the year 858, and was first applied to the region around the modern Kempten near Bingen. "Lei" means a rock; "Loreley" means then "Elbfels." And what Brentano and his followers have done is to apply the name of a place to a person.

In *Urania: Taschenbuch auf das Jahr 1821*, Graf von Loebcn published his "Loreley: Eine Sage vom Rhein." The following ballad introduces the saga in prose. Heine's ballad is set opposite for the sake of comparison.[32]

Da wo der Mondschein blitzet　　Ich weiss nicht, was soll es bedeuten
Um's hOechste Felsgestein,　　Dass ich so traurig bin;
Das ZauberfrAeulein sitzet　　Ein MAerchen aus alten Zeiten,
Und schauet auf den Rhein.　　Das kommt mir nicht aus dem Sinn.

Es schauet herUeber, hinUeber,　　Die Luft ist kUehl und es dunkelt,
Es schauet hinab, hinauf,　　Und ruhig fliesst der Rhein;
Die Schifflein ziehn vorUeber,　　Der Gipfel des Berges funkelt
Lieb' Knabe, sieh nicht auf!　　Im Abendsonnenschein.

Sie singt dir hold zum Ohre,　　Die schOenste Jungfrau sitzet
Sie blickt dich thOericht an,　　Dort oben wunderbar,
Sie ist die schOene Lore,　　Ihr goldenes Geschmeide blitzet,
Sie hat dir's angethan.　　Sie kAemmt ihr goldenes Haar.

Sie schaut wohl nach dem Rheine,　　Sie kAemmt es mit goldenem Kamme,
Als schaute sie nach dir,　　Und singt ein Lied dabei;
Glaub's nicht, dass sie dich meine,　　Das hat eine wundersame
Sich nicht, horch nicht nach ihr!　　Gewaltige Melodei.

So blickt sie wohl nach allen　　Den Schiffer im kleinen Schiffe
Mit ihrer Augen Glanz,　　Ergreift es mit wildem Weh;
LAesst her die Locken wallen　　Er schaut nicht die Felsenriffe,
Im wilden goldnen Tanz.　　Er schaut nur hinauf in die HOeh'.

Graf von Loeben and the Legend

Doch wogt in ihrem Blicke Ich glaube, die Wellen verschlingen
Nur blauer Wellen Spiel, Am Ende Schiffer und Kahn;
Drum scheu die WassertUecke, Und das hat mit ihrem Singen
Denn Flut bleibt falsch und kUehl! Die Lorelei gethan.

The following saga then relates how an old hunter sings this song to a young man in a boat on the Rhine, warning him against the allurements of the Lorelei on the rock above. The hunter's good intentions are fruitless, the young man is drowned.

In the autumn of 1823, Heine wrote, while at Luneburg, his "Die Lorelei." It was first published[33] in the *Gesellschafter,* March 26, 1824. Commentators refer to the verse, "Ein MAerchen aus alten Zeiten," as a bit of fiction, adding that it is not a title of olden times, but one invented by Brentano about 1800. The statement is true but misleading, for we naturally infer that Heine derived his initial inspiration from Brentano's ballad. Concerning this matter there are three points of view: Some editors and historians point out Brentano's priority and list his successors without committing[34] themselves as to intervening influence. This has only bibliographical value and for our purpose may be omitted. Some trace Heine's ballad direct to Brentano, some direct to Loeben. Which of these two points of view has the more argument in its favor and can there be still a third?

In the first place, Heine never knew Brentano personally, and never mentions him in his letters previous to 1824, nor in his letters[35] that have thus far been published after 1824. *Godwi* was repudiated soon after its publicatipn by Brentano himself, who said[36] there was only one good thing about it, the title, for, after people had said "Godwi," they could just keep on talking and say, "Godwi, dumm." On its account, Caroline called him Demens Brentano, while Dorothea dubbed him "Angebrenntano." The novel became a rare and unread book until Anselm Ruest brought out a new edition[37] with a critical and appreciative introduction in 1906. Diel and Kreiten say "es ging fast spurlos vorUeber." It was not included in his *Gesammelte Schriften* (1852–55), though the ballad[38] was. Heine does not mention it in his *Romantische Schule*, which was, however, written ten years after he had finished his "Die Lorelei." And as to the contents of Brentano's ballad, there is precious little in it that resembles Heine's ballad, aside from the name of the heroine, and even here the similarity is far from striking.

And yet, despite all this, commentators continue to say that Heine drew the initial inspiration for his "Lorelei" from Brentano. They may be right, but no one of them has

Graf von Loeben and the Legend

thus far produced any tenable argument, to say nothing of positive proof. The most recent supporter of Brentano's claim is Eduard Thorn[39] (1913), who reasons as follows:

Heine knew Brentano's works in 1824, for in that year he borrowed *Wunderhorn* and *TrOesteinsamkeit* from the library at GOettingen. These have, however, nothing to do with Brentano's ballad, and it is one year too late for Heine's ballad. All of Thorn's references to Heine's *Romantische Schule*, wherein *Godwi*, incidentally, is not mentioned, though other works are, collapse, for this was written ten years too late. And then, to quote Thorn: "Loeben's Gedicht lieferte das direkte Vorbild fUer Heine." He offers no proof except the statements of Strodtmann, Hessel, and Elster to this effect.

And again: "Der Name Lorelay findet sich bei Loeben nicht als Eigenname, wenn er auch das Gedicht, 'Der Lurleifels' Ueberschreibt." But the name Loreley does occur[40] twice on the same page on which the last strophe of the ballad is published in *Urania*, and here the ballad is not entitled "Der Lurleifels," but simply "Loreley." Now, even granting that Loeben entitled his ballad one way in the MS and Brockhaus published it in another way in *Urania*, it is wholly improbable that Heine saw Loeben's MS previous to 1823.

And then, after contending that Brentano's *RheinmAerchen*,[41] which, though written before 1823, were not published until 1846, must have given Heine the hair-combing motif, Thorn says: "Also kann nur Brentano das Vorbild geliefert haben." This cannot be correct. What is, on the contrary, at least possible is that Heine influenced Brentano.[42] The *RheinmAerchen* were finished, in first form, in 1816. And Guido GOerres, to whom Brentano willed them, and who first published them, tells us how Brentano carried them around with him in his satchel and changed them and polished them as opportunity was offered and inspiration came. It is therefore reasonable to believe that Heine helped Brentano to metamorphose his Lorelei of the ballad, where she is wholly human, into the superhuman Lorelei of the *RheinmAerchen* where she does, as a matter of fact, comb her hair with a golden comb.[43]

And now as to Loeben: Did Heine know and borrow from his ballad? Aside from the few who do not commit themselves, and those who trace Heine's poem direct to Brentano, and Oscar F. Walzel to be referred to later, all commentators, so far as I have looked into the matter, say that he did. Adolf Strodtmann said[44] it first (1868), in the following words: "Es leidet wohl keinen Zweifel, dass Heine dies Loeben'sche Ballade gekannt und bei Abfassung seiner Lorelei-Ballade benutzt hat." But he produces no proof except

Graf von Loeben and the Legend

similarity of form and content. Of the others who have followed his lead, ten, for particular reasons, should be authorities: Franz Muncker,[45] Karl Hessel,[46] Karl Goedeke,[47] Wilhelm Scherer,[48] Georg MUecke,[49] Wilhelm Hertz,[50] Ernst Elster,[51] Georg Brandes,[52] Heinrich Spiess,[53] and Herrn. Anders KrUeger.[54] But no one of them offers any proof except Strodtmann's statement to this effect.

Now their contention may be substantially correct; but their method of contending is scientifically wrong. To accept, where verification is necessary, the unverified statement of any man is wrong. And, that is the case here. Elster's note is of peculiar interest. He says: "Heine schloss sich am nAechsten an die Bearbeitung eines Stoffs an, die ein Graf LOeben 1821 verOeffentlichte." The expression "ein Graf LOeben" is grammatical evidence, though not proof, of one of two things: that Loeben was to Elster himself in 1890 a mere name, or that Elster knew Loeben would be this to the readers of his edition of Heine's works. Brandes says: "Die Nachahmung ist unzweifelhaft."[55] His proof is Strodtmann's statement, and similarity of content and form, with special reference to the two rhymes "sitzet–blitzet" that occur in both. But this was a very common rhyme with both Heine and Loeben in other poems. How much importance can be attached then to similarity of content and form?

The verse and strophe form, the rhyme scheme, the accent, the melody, except for Heine's superiority, are the same in both. As to length, the two poems are exactly equal, each containing, by an unimportant but interesting coincidence, precisely 117 words.[56] But the contents of the two poems are not nearly so similar as they apparently seemed, at first blush, to Adolf Strodtmann. The melodious singing, the golden hair and the golden comb and the use that is made of both, the irresistibly sweet sadness, the time, "Aus alten Zeiten," and the subjectivity—Heine himself recites his poem—these indispensable essentials in Heine's poem are not in Loeben's. Indeed as to content and of course as to merit, the two poems are far removed from each other.

And, moreover, literary parallels are the ancestors of that undocile child, Conjecture. We must remember that sirenic and echo poetry are almost as old as the tide of the sea, certainly as old as the hills, while as to the general situation, there is a passage in Milton's *Comus* (ll. 880–84) analogous to Heine's ballad, as follows:

And fair Ligea's golden comb,
Wherewith she sits on diamond rocks,

Graf von Loeben and the Legend

Sleeking her soft alluring locks,
By all the nymphs that nightly dance
Upon thy streams with wily glance,

and so on. And as to the pronounced similarity of form, we must remember that Heine was here employing his favorite measure, while Loeben was almost the equal of Ruckert in regard to the number of verse and strophe forms he effectively and easily controlled. In short, striking similarity in content is lacking, and as to the same sort of similarity in form to this but little if any significance can be attached.

And if the internal evidence is thin, the external is invisible, except for the fact that Loeben's ballad was published by Brockhaus, whom Heine knew by correspondence. But between the years 1818 and 1847, Heine never published anything in *Urania*,[57] which was used by so many of his contemporaries. Heine and Loeben never knew each other personally, and between the years 1821 and 1823 they were never regionally close together.[58] Heine never mentions Loeben in his letters; nor does he refer to him in his creative works, despite the fact that he had a habit of alluding to his brothers in Apollo, even in his poems.[59]

And therefore, though it is fashionable to say that Heine knew Loeben's ballad in 1823, and though the contention is plausible, it is impossible to prove it. Impossible also for this reason: Karl Simrock, Heine's intimate friend, included in his *Rheinsagen* (1836, 1837, 1841)[60] the ballads on the Lorelei by Brentano, Eichendorff, Heine, and himself. Why did he exclude the one by Loeben? He made an ardent appeal in his preface to his colleagues to inform him of any other ballads that had been written on these themes. The question must be referred to those who like to skate on flabby ice in things literary.

The most plausible theory in regard to the source of Heine's ballad is the one proposed by Oscar F. Walzel, who says: "Heine hat den Stoff wahrscheinlich aus dem ihm wohlbekannten *Handbuch fUer Reisende am Rhein* von Aloys Schreiber Uebernommen."[61] The only proof that Walzel gives that Heine knew Schreiber's manual is a reference[62] to it in *Lutetia*. But this was written in 1843, and proves nothing as to 1823. His contention, however, that Heine borrowed from Schreiber[63] has everything in its favor, from the point of view of both external and internal evidence and deserves, therefore, detailed elaboration.

Graf von Loeben and the Legend

As to internal evidence, there is only one slight difference between Heine's ballad and Schreiber's saga: where Heine's Lorelei combs her hair with a golden comb and has golden jewelry, Schreiber's "bindet einen Kranz fUer ihre goldenen Locken" and "hat eine Schnur von Bernstein in der Hand." Even here the color scheme is the same; otherwise there is no difference: time, place, and events are precisely the same in both. The mood and style are especially similar. The only words in Heine not found in Schreiber are "Kamm" and "bedeuten." Schreiber goes, to be sure, farther than does Heine: he continues the story after the death of the hero.[64] This, however, is of no significance, for Heine was simply interested in his favorite theme of unrequited or hindered love.

Now Heine must have derived his plot from somewhere, else this would be an uncanny case of coincidence. And the two expressions, "Aus alten Zeiten," and "Mit ihrem Singen," the latter of which is so important, Heine could have derived only from Schreiber. Heine was not jesting when he said it was a fairy tale from the days of old; he was following, it seems, Schreiber's saga, the first sentence of which reads as follows: "In alten Zeiten liess sich manchmal auf dem Lureloy um die AbenddAemmerung und beym Mondschein eine Jungfrau sehen, die mit so anmuthiger Stimme sang, dass alle, die es hOerten, davon bezaubert wurden." But Brentano's Lorelei does not sing at all, and Loeben's just a little, "Sie singt dir hold zum Ohre," while Heine, like Schreiber, puts his heroine in the prima donna class, and has her work her charms through her singing. And it seems that Heine was following Schreiber when the latter wrote as follows: "Viele, die vorUeberschifften, gingen am Felsenriff oder im Strudel zu Grunde, weil sie nicht mehr auf den Lauf des Fahrzeugs achteten, sondern von den himmlischen TOenen der wunderbaren Jungfrau gleichsam vom Leben abgelOest wurden, wie das zarte Leben der Blume sich im sUessen Duft verhaucht."

And as to her personal appearance, Brentano and Loeben simply tell us that she was beautiful, Brentano employing the Homeric method of proving her beauty by its effects. Heine and Schreiber not only comment upon her physical beauty, they also tell us how she enhanced her natural charms by zealously attending to her hair and her jewelry and religiously guarding the color scheme in so doing. In brief, the similarity is so striking that, if we can prove that Heine knew Schreiber in 1823, we can definitely assert that Schreiber[65] was his main, if not his unique, source.

Graf von Loeben and the Legend

Let us take up the various arguments in favor of the contention that Heine knew Schreiber's Handbuch in 1823, beginning with the least convincing. If Heine read Loeben's ballad and saga in "*Urania* fUer 1821," he could thereby have learned also of Schreiber's *Rheinsagen*, for, by a peculiar coincidence for our purpose, Brockhaus discusses[66] these in the introduction in connection with a tragedy by W. Usener, entitled Die BrUeder, and based upon one of Schreiber's *Sagen*. Proof, then, that Heine knew Loeben in 1823 is almost proof that he also knew Schreiber.

But there is better proof than this. In Elementargeister[67], we find this sentence: "Ganz genau habe ich die Geschichte nicht im Kopfe; wenn ich nicht irre, wird sie in Schreibers *Rheinischen Sagen* aufs umstAendlichste erzAehlt. Es ist die Sage vom Wisperthal, welches unweit Lorch am Rheine gelegen ist." And then Heine tells the same story that is told by Schreiber. It is the eighth of the seventeen *Sagen* in question. This, then, is proof that Heine knew Schreiber so long before 1835 that he was no longer sure he could depend upon his memory. But it is impossible to say whether Heine's memory was good for twelve years, or more, or less.

But there is better evidence than this. Heine's *Der Rabbi von Bacharach* reaches far back into his life. That he intended to write this sort of work before 1823 has been proved;[68] just when he actually began to write this particular work is not so clear, but we know that he did much preliminary reading by way of preparing himself for its composition. And the region around and above and below Bacharach comes in for detailed discussion and elaborate description in Schreiber's *Rheinsagen*. The crusades, the *Sankt-Wernerskirchen*, Lorch, the *Fischfang*, Hatto's *MAeuseturm*, the maelstrom at Bingen, the *Kedrich*, the story of the *Kecker Reuter* who liberated the maid that had been abducted by dwarfs, and again, and this is irrefutable, the story "von dem wunderlicheft Wisperthale drUeben, wo die VOegel ganz vernUenftig sprechen," all of these and others play a large role in Schreiber's sagas and in Heine's *Rabbi*. No one can read Schreiber's *Handbuch* and Heine's *Rabbi* without being convinced that the former stood sponsor for the latter.

And lastly, Heine wrote before 1821 his poem entitled "Die zwei BrUeder."[69] It is the tenth of the seventeen *Volkssagen* by Schreiber, the same theme as the one treated by W. Usener already referrred to. It is an old story,[70] and Heine could have derived his material from a number of places, but not from Grimm's *Deutsche Sagen*, indeed from no place so convenient as Schreiber. Heine knew Schreiber's *Handbuch*[71] in 1823.

Graf von Loeben and the Legend

The situation, then, is as follows: Heine had to have a source or sources, There are three candidates for Heine honors; Brentano, Loeben, Schreiber. Brentano has a number of supporters, though the evidence, external and internal, is wholly lacking. It would seem that lack of attention to chronology has misled investigators. Brentano's ballad can now be read in many places, but between about 1815 and 1823 it was safely concealed in the pages of an unread and unknown novel. Loeben[72] has many supporters, though the external evidence, except for the fact that Heine corresponded with Brockhaus, is wholly lacking, and the internal weakens on careful study. It would seem that the striking similarity in form has misled investigators. Schreiber has only one supporter, despite the fact that the evidence, external and internal, is as strong as it can be without Heine's ever having made some such remark as the following: "Yes, in 1823 I knew *only* Schreiber's saga and borrowed from it." But Heine never made any such statement. It would seem that the strong assertions of so many investigators in favor of Brentano and Loeben have made careful study of the matter appear not worth while; the problem was apparently solved. And since Heine never committed himself in this connection, the matter will, in all probability, remain forever conjectural. This much, however, is irrefutable: even if Heine knew in 1823 the five *Loreleidichtungen*, that had then been written, those by Brentano, Niklas Vogt, Eichendorff, Schreiber, and Loeben, and if he borrowed what he needed from all of them, he borrowed more from Schreiber[73] than from the other four combined.[74]

III

Whore Brentano sowed, many have reaped. Since the publication of his *Godwi*, about sixty–five *Loreleidichtungen*[75] have been written in German, the most important being those by Brentano (1810–16), Niklas Vogt[76] (1811), Eichendorff (*ca.* 1812), Loeben (1821), Heine (1823), Simrock (1837, 1840), Otto Ludwig (1838), Geibel (1834, 1846), W. MUeller von KOenigswinter (1851), Carmen Sylva, (*ca.* 1885), A. L'Arronge (1886), Julius Wolff (1886), and Otto Roquette (1889). In addition[77] to these, the story has been retold[78] many times, with slight alterations of the "original" versions, by compilers of chrestomathies, and parodies have been written on it. There is hardly a conceivable interpretation that has not been placed upon the legend.[79] The Lorelei has been made by some the evil spirit that entices men into hazardous games of chance, by others, she is the lofty incarnation of a desire to live and be blessed with the love that knows no turning away. The story has also wandered to Italy, France, England, Scotland,

Graf von Loeben and the Legend

Scandinavia, and the United States,[80] and the heroine has proved a grateful theme for painters and sculptors. Of the epic works, that by Julius Wolff is of interest because of the popularity it has enjoyed. First published in 1886, it had reached the forty-sixth thousand in 1898. Of the dramas that by L'Arronge should be valuable, but it has apparently never been published; nor has Otto Ludwig's operatic fragment,[81] unless recently. Aside from Geibel, Otto Roquette is the most interesting librettist. Of the forty-odd (there were forty-two in 1898) composers of Heine's ballad, the greatest are Schumann, Raff, and Liszt, and in this case Friedrich Sucher,[82] who married the ballad to its now undivorceable melody.

Though Brentano created[83] the story of his ballad, he located it in a region rich in legendary material, and it was the echo-motif of which he made especial use, and traces of this can be found in German literature as early as the thirteenth century.[84] The first real poet to borrow from Brentano was Eichendorff,[85] in whose *Ahnung und Gegenwart* we have the poem since published separately under the title of "WaldgesprAech," and familiar to many through Schumann's composition.[86] That Eichendorff's Lorelei operates the forest is only to be expected of the author of so many *Waldlieder*. Even if Heine had known it he could have borrowed nothing from it except the name of his heroine.[87]

As to Loeben's saga, there can be but little doubt that he derived his initial inspiration from Schreiber, with whom he became intimately acquainted[88] at Heidelberg during the winter of 1807-8. This, of course, is not to say that Heine borrowed from Loeben. Indeed, one of the strongest proofs that Heine borrowed from Schreiber rather than from Loeben is the clarity and brevity, ease and poetry of Schreiber's saga as over against the obscurity and diffuseness, clumsiness and woodenness of Loeben's saga,[89] the plot of which, so far as the action is concerned, is as follows: Hugbert von Stahleck, the son of the Palsgrave, falls in love with the Lorelei and rows out in the night to her seat by the Rhine. In landing, he falls into the stream, the Lorelei dives after him and brings him to the surface. The old Palsgrave has, in the meanwhile, sent a knight and two servants to capture the Lorelei. They climb the lofty rock and hang a stone around the enchantress' neck, when she voluntarily leaps from the cliff into the Rhine below and is drowned.

The one episode in Loeben not found in any of Schreiber's *Rheinsagen* is the story of the castaway ring miraculously restored from the stomach of the fish. This Loeben could have taken from "Magelone" by Tieck, or "Polykrates" by Schiller, both of whom he

Graf von Loeben and the Legend

revered as men and with whose works he was thoroughly familiar. But there is nothing in Loeben that Heine could not have derived in more inspiring form from Schreiber; and Schreiber contains essentials not in Loeben at all. Indeed, a general study of Schreiber's manuals leads one to believe that the influence of them, as a whole, on Heine would be a most grateful theme: there is not one Germanic legend referred to in Heine that is not contained in Schreiber. And as a prose writer, Heine's fame rests largely on his travel pictures.[90]

The points of similarity between Loeben's ballad and saga and the ballads and MAerchen of Brentano, all of which Loeben knew in 1821, are wholly negligible. It remains,[91] therefore, simply to point out some of the peculiarities of Brentano's "Loreley" as protrayed in the *RheinmAerchen*—peculiarities that are interesting in themselves and that may have played a part in the development of the legend since 1846.

In "Das MAerchen von dem Rhein und dem MUeller Radlauf,"[92] Loreley is portrayed in a sevenfold capacity, as it were: seven archways lead to seven doors that open onto seven stairways that lead to a large hall in which Frau Lureley sits on a sevenfold throne with seven crowns upon her head and her seven daughters around her. This makes interesting reading for children, but Brentano did not lose sight of adults, including those who like to speculate as to the origin of the legend. He says: "Sie [Lorelei] ist eine Tochter der Phantasie, welches eine berUehmte Eigenschaft ist, die bei Erschaffung der Welt mitarbeitete und das Allerbeste dabei that; als sie unter der Arbeit ein schOenes Lied sang, hOerte sie es immer wiederholen und fand endlich den Wiederhall, einen schOenen JUengling in einem Felsen sitzen, mit dem sie sich verheiratete und mit ihm die Frau Lureley erzeugte; sie hatten auch noch viele andere Kinder, zum Beispiel: die Echo, den Akkord, den Reim, deren Nachkommen sich noch auf der Welt herumtreiben."

Just as Frau Lureley closes the first *MAerchen*, so does she begin the second: "Von dem Hause Staarenberg und den Ahnen des MUellers Radlauf."[93] Here she creates, or motivates, the other characters. Her seven daughters appear with her, as follows: Herzeleid, Liebesleid, Liebeseid, Liebesneid, Liebesfreud, Reu und Leid, and Mildigkeit. She reappears then with her seven daughters at the close of the *MAerchen*, and each sings a beautiful song, while Frau Lureley, the mother of Radlauf, proves to be a most beneficent creature. Imaginative as Brentano was, he rarely rose to such heights as in this and the next, "MAerchen vom Murmelthier,"[94] in which Frau Lureley continues her great work of love and kindness. She rights all wrongs, rewards the just, corrects the

Graf von Loeben and the Legend

unjust, and leads a most remarkable life whether among the poor on land or in her element in the water. All of which is poles removed from Loeben's saga, though he knew these *MAerchen*,[95] for they were written when Brentano was his intimate friend.

As to the importance of Loeben's saga, Wilhelm Hertz says: "Fast alle jUengeren Dichter knUepfen an seinen Erfindungen an, so besonders die zahlreichen musikdramatischen Bearbeitungen."[96] It is extremely doubtful that this statement is correct. It is plain that many of the lyric writers leaned on Schreiber, and the librettists could have done the same; or they could have derived their initial suggestion in more attractive form than that offered by Loeben. It seems, however, that Geibel[97] knew Loeben's saga. Though his individual poems on the Lorelei betray the influence of Heine, and though his drama resembles Brentano's ballad in mood and in unimportant details, it contains the same proper names of persons and places that are found in Loeben. And what is more significant, it contains two important events that are not found in any of the other versions of the saga: the scene with the wine-growers and the story of the castaway ring. The latter is an old theme, but that they both occur in Loeben and in Geibel would argue that the latter took them from the former. It is largely a question as to whether a poet like Geibel has to have a source for everything that is not absolutely abstract. The entire matter is complicated.[98] The paths of the Lorelei have crossed each other many times since Brentano started her on her wanderings. To draw up a map of her complete course, showing just who influenced whom, would be a task more difficult than grateful.[99]

As to Brentano's original ballad,[100] try as we may to depreciate the value of his creation by tracing it back to echo-poetry and by coupling it with older legends, such as that of Frau Holla, we are forced to give him credit for having not simply revived but for having created a legend that is beautiful in itself and that has found a host of imitators, direct and indirect, the world over, including one of the world's greatest lyric writers. This then is just one of the many things that the German romanticists started; it is just one of their many contributions to the literature that lasts. And for the perpetuation of this one, students of German literature have, it seems, given the obscure Graf von Loeben entirely too much credit. But who will give the oft-scolded Clemens Brentano too little credit? Only those who dislike romanticism on general principles and who will not be convinced that the romanticists could be original.[101]

ALLEN WILSON PORTERFIELD

Graf von Loeben and the Legend

COLUMBIA UNIVERSITY

NEW YORK CITY

FOOTNOTES:

[1] Ferdinand August Otto Heinrich Graf von Loeben, the scion of an old, aristocratic, Protestant family, was born at Dresden, August 18, 1786. He received his first instruction from private tutors. For three years from 1804 on, he unsuccessfully, because unwillingly, studied law at the University of Wittenberg. In 1807 he entered, to his profound delight, the University of Heidelberg, where, in association with Arnim, Brentano, and GOerres, he satisfied his longing for literature and art. Beginning with 1808 he lived alternately at Wien, Dresden, and Berlin and with Fouque at Nennhausen. He took an active part in the campaign of 1813–14, marched to Paris, and returned after his company had been disbanded, to Dresden, where, in 1817, he married Johanna Victoria Gottliebe *geb.* von Bressler and established there his permanent abode. In 1822 he suffered a stroke of apoplexy from which he never recovered: even the magnetic treatment given him by Justinus Kerner proved of no avail. He died at Dresden, April 3, 1825. See *Allgemeine deutsche Biographie*, XIX, 40–45. The article is by Professor Muncker. Wilhelm MUeller also wrote an article full of lavish praise of Loeben in *Neuer Nekrolog der Deutschen*, III, Jahrg. 1824, Ilmenau, 1827.

[2] Meyer (6th ed.) does not mention Loeben even in the articles on Fouque and Malsburg, two of Loeben's best friends; Brockhaus (Jubilee ed.) mentions him as one of Eichendorff's friends in the article on Eichendorff, but neither has an independent note on Loeben. Nor is he mentioned in such compendious works on the nineteenth century as those by Gottschall, R.M. Meyer (*Grundriss* and *Geschichte*), and Fr. Kummer. Biese says (*Deutsche Literaturgeschichte*, II. 436) of him: "Auch

ein so ausgesprochenes Talent, wie es Graf von Loeben war, entging nicht der Gefahr, die Romantik in ihre Karikatur zu verzerren."

[3] Cf. *Allgemeine deutsche Biographie*, XIX, 42.

[4] Partial lists of his works are given in: Goedeke, *Grundriss*, VI, 108–10 (2nd ed.): *Allgemeine deutsche Biographie*, XIX. 40–45; the sole monograph on Loeben by Raimund Pissin. *Otto Heinrich Graf von Loeben, sein Leben und seine Werke*, Berlin, 1905, 326 pages. By piecing these lists together—for they vary—it seems that Loeben wrote, aside from the works mentioned above, the following: 1 conventional drama, 1 musical-romantic drama, 2 narrative poems, one of which is on Ferdusi, 3 collections of poems, between 30 and 40 novelettes, fairy tales and so on. and "einige tausend" aphorisms and detached thoughts. It is in Pissin's monograph that Loeben's position in the Heidelberg circle of 1807–8 is worked out. as follows: Loeben and Eichendorff constituted one branch, Arnim and Brentano the other, GOerres stood loosely between the two, and the others sided now with one group, now with the other.

[5] The verses are from *GestAendnisse*, No. 125 in Pissin's collection of Loeben's poems.

[6] *GestAendnisse*. No. 125.

[7] Aside from the reviews, letters, and individual poems reprinted here and there, the following works were accessible to the writer: (1) *Das weisse Ross, eine altdeutsche Familienchronik;* (2) *Die Sonnenkinder, eine ErzAehlung;* (3) *Die Perle und die Maiblume, eine Novelle;* (4) *Cephalus und Procris, ein Drama;* (5) *Ferdusi;* (6) *Persiens Ritter, eine ErzAehlung;* (7) *Die ZaubernAechte am Bosporus, ein romantisches Gedicht;* (8) *Prinz Floridio, ein MAerchen;* (9) *Leda; eine ErzAehlung;* (10) *WeinmAerchen;* (11) *GesAenge*.

Graf von Loeben and the Legend

[8] Eichendorff's relation to Loeben can be studied in the edition of Eichendorff's works by Wilhelm Kusch, Regensburg. Vols. III, X–XIII have already appeared. For a poetization of Loeben, see *Ahnung und Gegenwart*, chap. xii, pp. 144 ff. For a historical account of Loeben, see *Erlebtes*, chap. x, pp. 425 ff. It is here that Eichendorff makes Goethe praise Loeben in the foregoing fashion.

[9] There is no positive evidence that Goethe made any such remark. In his *GesprAeche* (Biedermann. V, 270; VI, 198–99) there are two references to Loeben by Goethe; they are favorable but noncommittal as to his poetic ability.

[10] Cf. *Die TagebUecher des GrAefen von Platen*, Stuttgart, 1900. Under date of August 14, 1824, Platen wrote: "Es enthAelt viele gute Bemerkungen, wiewohl diese Art Prosa nicht nach meinem Sinne ist." The reference is to Loeben's commentary to Madame de Staels *De l'Allemayne*.

[11] Cf. *Heinrick von Kleists Berliner KAempfe*, Berlin, 1901, pp. 490–96. The story in question is "Die furchtbare Einladung."

[12] Cf. *Herm. Anders KrUeger, Pseudoromantik. Friedrich Kind und der Dresdener Liederkreis. Leipzig. 1904. pp. 144–48*. KrUeger also discusses Loeben in his *Der junge Eichendorff. Leipzig. 1904. pp. 88 and 128*.

[13] Cf. Fouque, Apel. Miltitz. *BeitrAege zur Geschichte der deutschen Romantik*, Leipzig,1908. In a letter to his brother. Fouque wrote (January 6, 1813): "Ein Dichter, meine ich, ist er allerdings, ein von Gott dazu bestimmter." Fouque, however, realized Loeben's many weaknesses as a poet, though at Loeben's death he wrote a poem on him praising him as the master of verse technique.

[14] Cf. Kosch's edition of Eichendorff. XIII. 65. Loeben says: "In Weimar war ich im vorigen Winter bei Goethe; er war mir

freundlich." The "previous winter" was 1813.

[15] Cf. Kosch's edition, XI, 220. The remark was made in 1807.

[16] Cf. Pissin. p. 25. The incident occurred in 1803 and Herder died in 1804.

[17] Cf. Kosch's edition, XI, 308. Lochen himself utterly condemned this work later. See Pissin, pp. 238–39, 267–08. Pissin gives the number of verse and strophe forms on p. 266.

[18] Cf. Pissin, p. 267. Uhland made the remark in 1812—his own most fruitful year as a poet.

[19] The story was published in 1817. The full title is *Das weisse Ross, eine altdeutsche Familienchronik in sechs und dreissig Bildern.* It is 160 pages long.

[20] An idea as to the lack of action in this story can be derived from the following statement by Otto (pp. 127–28), the brave hero: "Was man Schicksale zu nennen pflegt, habe ich wenige gehabt, aber erfahren habe ich dennoch viel und mehr als mancher durch seine glAenzenden Schicksale erfahren mag: nAemlich die FUehrungen der ewigen Liebe habe ich erfahren, die keinen verlAesst. und alles herrlich hinausfuhrt." And then Siegenot, the other hero, says that this is very true—whereupon they embrace each other.

[21] The story was first published In Urania: Taschenbuch fUer Damen auf das Jahr 1818. pp. 305–37.

[22] Aside from the poems in Pissin's collection in the *D.L.D. des 18. u. 19. Jahr.*, Ignaz Hub's *Deutschlands Balladen–und Romanzen–Dichter*, Karlsruhe, 1845, contains: (1) "Romanze von der weissen Rose," (2) "Der Tanz mit dem Tode," (3) "Der Bergknapp," (4) "Das Schwanenlied." "Loreley" is also reprinted here, with modifications for the worse. "Schau', Schiffer, schau' nicht

Graf von Loeben and the Legend

hinauf," is certainly not an improvement on Loeben's "Lieb Knabe, sieh' nicht hinauf,"

[23] The following are common forms: "Nez," "zwey," "versteken," "SfAeren," "Saffo," "Stralenboten," "Abendrothen." "Uebermuth," and so on, though the regular forms, except in the case of "Saffo," also occur.

[24] "Der Abend" reminds one strongly of HOelderlin's "Die Nacht," while "Tag und Nacht" goes back undoubtedly to Novalis' "Hymnen an die Nacht," W. Schlegels sonnet on the sonnet stood sponsor for "Das Sonett," and Goethe and Tieck also reoccur in changed dress. The poems on Correggio (73), Ruisdael (75), Goethe (137), Tieck (138–39), and Novalis (141) sound especially like W. Schlegel's poems on other poets and artists.

[25] In his *Geschichte des Sonettes in der deutschen Dichtung.*'Leipzig, 1884. Heinrich Weltl (pp. 210–17) criticizes Loeben's sonnets most severely from the point of view of content; and as to their form he says: "Blos die Form, oder gar die blosse Form der Form ist beachtenswert." This is unquestionably a case of warping the truth in order to bring in a sort of pun.

[26] The triolett is worth quoting as a type of Loeben's prettiness:

Galt es mir, das sUesse Blicken Aus dem hellen Augenpaar? Unter'm Netz vom goldnen Haar Galt es mir das sUesse Blicken? Einem sprach es von Gefahr, Einen wollt' es licht umstricken; Galt es mir, das sUesso Blicken Aus dem hellen Augenpaar.

[27] An idea as to Loeben's temperament can he derived from the following passage in a letter to Tieck: "Gott sei mit Ihnen und die heilige Muse! Oft drAengt es mich, niederzuknien im Schein, den Albrecht DUerers und Novalis Glorie wirft, im alten frommen Dom. dann denk' ich Ihrer und ich lieg' an Ihrer Seele. Ich fUehle Sie in mir, wie man eine Gottheit fUehlt in geweihter Stunde. 'Liebe denkt in sel'gen TOenen, denn Gedanken stehn zu

fern." The quotation should read "sUessen" instead of "sel'gen." See *Briefe an Tierk.* edited by Holtei, II, 266.

[28] As a corrective to the monographs of Pissin on Loeben and H. A. KrUeger on Eichendorff. one should read Wilhelm Kosch's article in *Euphorion* (1907, pp. 310–20). Kosch. contends that Pissin and KrUeger have vastly overestimated Loeben's influence on Eichendorff, and that Loeben in general was "eine bedeutungslose Tageserscheinung."

[29] The complete title is *Godwi, oder das steinerne Bild der Mutter. Ein verwilderter Roman von Maria.* The very rare first edition of this novel, in two volumes, is in the Columbia Library. Friedrich Wilmans was the publisher.

[30] Cf. Alfred Kerr, *Godwi. Ein Kapitel deutscher Romantik.* Berlin, 1898, p. 2.

[31] Cf. Wilhelm Hertz, "UEber den Namen Lorelei," *Sitzungsberichte der k.b. Akademie der Wissenschaften zu MUenchen*, Jahrgang 1886, pp. 217–51. For the etymologist, this is an invaluable study.

[32] The superficial similarity of those two poems can easily be exaggerated. The rhyme "sitzet–blitzet" is perfectly natural: the Lorelei had to be portrayed as "sitzen"; what is then easier than "blitzen"? In "Ritter Peter von Stauffenberg und die Meerfeye" (Des Knaben Wunderhorn, ed. of Eduard Grisebach, p. 277) we have this couplet:

Er sieht ein schOenes Weib da sitzen. Von Gold und Silber herrlich blitzen.

For more detailed illustrations, see below.

[33] It is worth while to note the actual date of Heine's composition of his ballad, since so eminent an authority as Wilhelm Scherer

(*Ges. d. deut. Lit.*, 8th ed., p. 662) says that Heine wrote the
poem in 1824. And Eduard Thorn (*Heinrich Heines Beziehungen zu
Clemens Brentano*, p. 90.) says that he published it in 1826.
This is incorrect, as is also Thorn's statement, p. 88, that
Brentano wrote his ballad in 1802. For the correct date of Heine's
ballad, see *SAemtliche Werke*, Hamburg, 1865, XV, 200.]

[34] An instance of this is seen in *Selections from Heine's
Poems*, edited by H.S. White, D.C. Heath &Co., Boston, 1900,
p. 182. Professor White does, to be sure, refer to Strodtmann for
the details; but Strodtmann does not prove anything. And in
Heines Werke in fUenfzehn Teilen, edited by Hermann
Friedeman, Helene Herrmann. Erwin Kaliseher. Raimund Pissin, and
Veit Valentin, we have the comment by Helene Herrmann, who follows
Pissin: "Die Loreleysage, erfunden von Clemens Brentano; vielfach
von Romantikern gestaltet. Zwischen Brentanos Romanze und Heines
Situationsbild steht die Behandlung durch den Grafen Loeben, einen
unbedeutenden romantischen Dichter."

[35] The best finished collection of Heine's letters is the one by
Hans Daffis, Berlin, 1907, 2 vols. This collection will, however,
soon be superseded by *Heinrich Heines Briefwechsel*, edited
by Friedrich Hirth, MUenchen and Berlin, 1914. The first volume
covers Heine's life up to 1831. In neither of these collections is
either Brentano or Loeben mentioned. There are 643 pages in
Hirth's first volume.

[36] For a discussion of *Godwi*, see *Clemens Brentano: Ein
Lebensbild*, by Johannes Baptista Diel and Wilhelm Kreiten,
Freiburg i.B., 1877, two volumes in one, pp. 104–25. As to the
obscurity of Brentano's work, one sentence (p. 116) is
significant: "*Godwi* spukt heutzutage nur mehr in den KOepfen
der liberalen Literaturgeschichtsschreiber, denen er einen
willkommenen Vorwand an die Hand gibt, mit einigen stereotyp
abgeschriebenen Phrasen den Stab Ueber den phantastischen,
verschwommenen, unsittlichen u.s.w., u.s.w. Dichter zu brechen."

Graf von Loeben and the Legend

[37] *Clemens Brentano: Godwi oder das steinerne Bild der Mutter. Ein verwilderter. Roman.* Herausgegeben und eingeleitet von Dr. Anselm Ruest, Berlin, 1906. Ruest edited the work because he thought it was worth reviving. In this edition, the ballad is on pages 507–10. Bartels (Handbuch, 2d ed., p. 400) lists a reprint in 1905, E.A. Regener, Berlin.

[38] II, 391–93.

[39] For the various references, see Thorn's *Heinrich Heines Beziehungen zu Clemens Brentano.* pp. 88–90. His study is especially unsatisfactory in view of the fact that he says (p. 88) in this connection: "Wirklich Neues zu bringen ist uns nicht vergOennt, denn selbstverstAendlich haben die Forscher dieses dankbare und interessante Objekt schon in der eingehendsten Weise untersucht." And Thorn's attempt to show that Heine knew *Godwi* early in life by pointing out similarities between poems in it and poems by Heine is about as untenable as argument could be, in view of the great number of poets who may have influenced Heine in these instances; Thorn himself lists (p. 63) BUerger, Fouque, Arnim, E.T.A. Hoffmann.

[40] In Pissin's collection of Loeben's poems (*D.L.D.*, No. 135) we have a peculiar note. After the ballad (*Anmerk.*, p. 161), which Pissin entitles "Der Lurleifels," we read: "N.d. Hs." This would argue that Loeben did so entitle his ballad and that Pissin had access to the original MS. But then Pissin says: "Auch, die gleichnamige Novelle einleitend, in der *Urania* auf 1821." But in *Urania* the novelette is entitled "Eine Sage vom Rhein." and the ballad is entitled "Loreley." Bet him who can unravel this!

[41] For the entire story of the composition and publication of the *RheinmAerchen*, see *Die MAerchen von Clemens Brentano*, edited by Guido GOerres. 2 vols. in 1, Stuttgart, 1879 (2d ed.) This edition contains the preface to the original edition of 1840,

Graf von Loeben and the Legend

pp. i–l.

[42] Thorn, who drew on M.R. Hewelcke's *Die Loreleisage*,
Paderborn, 1908, makes (p. 90) this suggestion. It is impossible
for the writer to see how Thorn can be so positive in regard to
Brentano's influence on Heine. And one's faith is shaken by this
sentence on the same page: "Brentano verOeffentlichte sein
Radlauf–MAerchen erst 1827, Heine 'Die Lorelei' schon 1826."
Both of these dates are incorrect. Guido GOerres, who must be
considered a final authority on this matter, says that, though
Brentano tried to publish his *MAerchen* as early as 1816,
none of them were published until 1846, except extracts from "Das
MyrtenfrAeulein," and a version of "Gockel," neither of which bears
directly on the Lorelei–matter.

[43] Of GOerres' second edition, I, 250: "Nachdem Murmelthier herzlich
fUer diese Geschenke gedankt hatte, sagte Frau Else: 'Nun, mein
Kind! kAemme mir und Frau Lurley die Haare, wir wollen die deinigen
dann auch kAemmen'—dann gab sie ihr einen goldnen Kamm, und
Murmelthier kAemmte Beiden die Haare und flocht sie so schOen, dass
die Wasserfrauen sehr zufrieden mit ihr waren."

[44] In *H. Heines Leben und Werke*. Hamburg, 1884 (3d ed.),
Bd. I. p. 363. In the notes, Strodtmann reprints Loeben's ballad,
pp. 696–97. His statement is especially unsatisfactory in view of
the fact that he refers to the "fast gleicher Inhalt," though the
essentials of Heine's ballad are not in Loeben's, and to
"einegewisse AEhnlichkeit in Form," though the similarity in form
is most pronounced.

[45] In *Allgemeine deut. Biog.*, XIX. 44. It is interesting to
see how Professor Muncker lays stress on this matter by placing in
parentheses the statement: "Einige ZUege der letzten Geschichte
["Sage vom Rhein"] regten Heine zu seinem bekannten Liede an."

Graf von Loeben and the Legend

[46] In *Dichtungen von Heinrich Heine, ausgewAehlt und erlAeutert*, Bonn, 1887, p. 326. Hessel's Statement is peculiarly unsatisfactory, since he says (p. 309) that he is going to the sources of Heine's poems, and then, after reprinting Loeben's ballad, he says: "Dieses Lied war Heines nAechstes Vorbild. AusfUehrlicheres bei Strodtmann, Bd. I, S. 362." And this edition has been well received.

[47] In *Grundriss, VI, 110. Again we read in parentheses: "Aus diesem Liede und dem EingAenge der ErzAehlung schOepfte H. Heine sein Lied von der Loreley."*

[48] In *Ges. d. deut. Lit.*, p. 662 (8th ed.).

[49] In *Heinrich Heines Beziehungen zum deutschen Mittelalter*, Berlin, 1908, pp., 94–95. MUecke is the most cautious of the ten authorities above listed; and he anticipated Walzel in his reference to Schreiber's *Handbuch*.

[50] In *Ueber den Namen Lorelei, p. 224. Hertz is about as cautious as Strodtmann; "Es ist kaum zu bezweifeln dass," etc.*

[51] In *SAemtliche Werke*, I, 491.

[52] In *HauptstrOemungen*. VI, 178. Brandes says: "Der Gegenstand ist der gleiche, das Versmass ist dasselbe, ja die Reimen sind an einzelnen Stellen die gleichen: blitzetsitzet; statt 'an–gethan' steht da nur 'Kahn–gethan.'"

[53] In *Der deutschen Romantiker*, Leipzig, 1903, p. 235.

[54] In *Deutsches Literatur–Lexikon*, MUenchen, 1914, p. 271. It is significant that KrUeger makes this statement, for the subtitle of his book Is "Biographisches und bibliographisches Handbuch mit MotivUebersichten und Quellennachweisen." And it is, on the whole, an extremely useful book.

Graf von Loeben and the Legend

[55] It is impossible to see how Brandes can lay great stress on the fact that this rhyme occurs in both poems. The following rhymes are found on the following pages of the Elster edition, Vol. I, of Heine's works: "Spitze–Blitze" (36), "sitzen–nUetzen" (116), "Witzen–nUetzen" (124), "sitzen–blitzen" (216), "erhitzet–bespitzet" (242), "Blitz–Sitz" (257), "blitzt–gestUetzt" (276), "blitze–besitze" (319), "blitzet–gespitzet" (464). And in Loeben's poems the rhyme is equally common. The first strophe of his *Ferdusi* runs as follows:

Hell erglAenzt an Persiens Throne Wo der grosse Mahmud sitzt; Welch Juwel ist's, das die Krone So vor allen schOen umblitzt.

And in Schreiber's saga we have in juxtaposition, the words. "Blitze" and "Spitze." The rhyme "Sitze–Blitze" occurs in Immanuel's "Lorelei," quoted by Seeliger, p. 31.

[56] There are, to be sure, only 114 words in Loeben's ballad if we count "um's," "dir's," and "glaub's" as three words and not six.

[57] These numbers are in the Columbia Library.

[58] During these years Heine's letters are dated from GOettingen, Berlin, Gnesen, Berlin, MUenster, Berlin, LUeneburg, Hamtburg, RitzenbUettel, and LUeneburg. During these same years Loeben was in Dresden and he was ill.

[59] We need only to mention such a strophe as the following from *Atta Troll*:

Klang das nicht wie JugendtrAeume. Die ich trAeumte mit Chamisso Und Brentano und Fouque In den blauen MondscheinnAechten?

See Elster edition, II, 421. The lines were written in 1843.

Graf von Loeben and the Legend

[60] The first edition of Karl Simrock's *Rheinsagen* came out in 1836. This was not accessible. The edition of 1837, "zweite, vermehrte Auflage," contains 168 poems, 572 pages; this contains Simrock's "Ballade von der Lorelei." The edition of 1841 also contains Simrock's "Der Teufel und die Lorelei." The book contains 455 pages, 218 poems. The sixth edition (1809) contains 231 poems. In all editions the poems are arranged in geographical order from SUedersee to GraubUenden. Alexander Kaufmann's *Quellenangaben und Bemerkungen zu Kart Simrocks Rheinsagen* throws no new light on the Lorelei-legend.

[61] Cf. *Heinrich Heines sAemtliche Werke*, edited by Walzel, FrAenkel, KrAehe, Leitzmann, and Peterson. Leipzig. 1911, II, 408. So far as I have looked into the matter, Walzel stands alone in this belief, though MUecke, as has been pointed out above, anticipated him in the statement that Heine drew on Schreiber in this case. But MUecke thinks that Heine also knew Loeben.

[62] The reference in question reads as follows: "Ich will kein Wort verlieren Ueber den Wert dieses unverdaulichen Machwerkes [*Les Burgraves*], das mit allen mOeglichen PrAetensionen auftritt, namentlich mit historischen, obgleich alles Wissen Victor Hugos Ueber Zeit und Ort, wo sein StUeck spielt, lediglich aus der franzOesischen Uebersetzung von Schreibers *Handbuch fUer Rheinreisende* geschOepft, ist." This was written March 20, 1843 (see Elster edition, VI. 344).

[63] Aloys Wilhelm Schreiber (1763–1840) was a teacher in the Lyceum at Baden–Baden (1800–1802), professor of aesthetics at Heidelberg (1802–13) where he was intimate with the Voss family, historiographer at Karlsruhe (1813–26), and in 1826 he retired and became a most prolific writer. He interested himself in guidebooks for travelers. His manuals contain maps, distances, expense accounts, historical sketches, in short, about what the modern *Baedeker* contains with fewer statistics and more popular description. His books appeared in German, French, and

Graf von Loeben and the Legend

English. In 1812 he published his *Handbuch fUer Reisende am Rhein von Schaffhausen bis Holland*, to give only a small part of the wordy title, and in 1818 he brought out a second, enlarged edition of the same work with an appendix containing 17 *Volkssagen aus den Gegenden am Rhein und am Taunus*, the sixteenth of which is entitled "Die Jungfrau auf dem Lurley." His books were exceedingly popular in their day and are still obtainable. Of the one here in question, Von Weech (*Allgem. deut. Biog.*, XXXII, 471) says: "Sein *Handbuch fUer Reisende am Rhein*, dessen Anhang eine wertvolle Sammlung rheinischer Volkssagen enthAelt, war lange der beliebteste FUehrer auf Rheinreisen." There are 7 volumes of his manuals in the New York Public Library, and one, *Traditions populaires du Rhin,* Heidelberg, 1830 (2d ed.), is in the Columbia Library. It contains 144 legends and beautiful engravings. (The writer has just [October 15, 1915] secured the four Volumes of Schreiber's *Rheinische Geschichten und Sagen*. The fourth volume, published in 1830. is now a very rare book.)

[64] The remainder of Schreiher's plot is as follows: The news of the infatuated hero's death so grieved the old Count that ho determined to have the Lorelei captured, dead or alive. One of his captains, aided by a number of brave followers, set out on the hazardous expedition. First, they surround the rock on which the Lorelei sits, and. then three of the most courageous ascend to her seat and determine to kill her, so that the danger of her repealing her former deed maybe forever averted. But when they reach her and she hoars what they intend to do, she simply smiles and invokes the aid of her Father, who immediately sends two white horses—two white waves—up the Rhine, and. after leaping down to the Rhine, she is safely carried away by these. She was never again seen, but her voice was frequently heard as she mocked, in echo, the songs of the sailors on her paternal stream.

[65] It is not simply in the appendix of Schreiber's *Handbuch* that he discusses the legend of Lorelei, but also in the

Graf von Loeben and the Legend

scientific part of it. Concerning the Lorelei rock he says
(pp. 174–75): "Ein wunderbarer Fels schiebt sich jetzt dem
Schiffer gleichsam in seine Bahn—es ist der Lurley (von Lure,
Lauter, und Ley, Schiefer) aus welchem ein Echo den Zuruf der
Vorbeifahrendem fUenfzehnmal wiederholt. Diesen Schieferfels
bewohnte in grauen Zeiten eine Undine, welche die Schiffenden
durch ihr Zurufen ins Verderben lockte."

[66] Brockhaus says (p. xxiv): "Die einfache Sage von den beiden
feindlichen BrUedern am Rhein, van denen die TrUemmer ihrer BUergen
selbst noch *Die BrUeder* heissen ist in A. Schreiber's
Auswahl von Sagen jener Gegenden zu lesen." Usener's tragedy is
published In full in this number of *Urania*, pp. 383–442.

[67] Cf. Elster edition, IV, 406–9. The circumstantial way in which
Heine retells this story is almost sufficient to lead one to
believe that he had Schreiber at hand when he wrote this part of
Elementargeister; but he says that he did not.

[68] Discussion as to the first conception of Heine's *Rabbi* are
found in: *Heinrich Heines Fragment*; *Der Rabbi von Bacharach*,
by Lion Feuchtwanger, MUenchen, 1907; *Heinrich Heine und Der Rabbi
von Bacharach*, by Gustav Karpeles, Wien, 1895.

[69] The poem is one of the *Junge Leiden*, published in 1821, Elster
(I, 490) says: "Eine bekannte Sage, mit einzelnen vielfach
wiederkehrenden uralten ZUegen, dargestellt In Simrocks
Rheinsagen." Simrock had, of course, done nothing on the
Rheinsagen in 1821, being then only nineteen years old and an
inconspicuous student at Bonn. Walzel says (I. 449.): "Mit einem
andern Ausgang ist die Sage in dem von Heine vielbenutzten
Handbuch fUer Reisende am Rhein von Aloys Schreiber (Heidelberg,
1816) Ueberliefert." The edition of this work in the New York
Public Library has no printed date, but 1818 is written in. Walzel
may be correct. The outcome of Heine's poem is, after all, not so
different: In Schreiber, both brothers relinquish their claims to

Graf von Loeben and the Legend

the girl and remain unmarried; in Heine the one kills the other and in this way neither wins the girl.

[70] It is the same story as the one told by Bulwer-Lytton in his *Pilgrims of the Rhine*. chap. xxiv.

[71] All through the body of Schreiber's *Handbuch*, there are references to the places and legends mentioned in Heine's *Rabbi*. On Bacharach there is the following: "Der Reisende, wenn er auch nur eine Stunde in Bacharach verweilt, unterlasse nicht, die Ruinen von Staleck zu besteigen, wo eine der schOensten Rheinlandschaften sich von seinen Blicken aufrollt. Die Burg von sehr betrAechtlichem Umfang scheint, auf den TrUemmern eines ROemerkastells erbaut. Die, welche die Entstehung derselben den Hunnen zuschreiben, well sie in Urkunden den Namen Stalekum hat, sind in einem Irrtum befangen, denn Stalekum oder Stalek heisst eben so viel als StalbUehl, oder ein Ort, wo ein Gericht gehegt wurde. Pfalzgraf Hermann von Staleck, starb im 12ten Jahrhundert; er war der letzte seines Stammes, und von ihm kam die Burg, als KOelnisches Lehen, an Konrad Von Staufen."

[72] To come back to Heine and Loeben, Herm. Anders KrUeger says (p., 147) in his *Pseudoromantik:* "Heinrich Heine, der Ueberhaupt Loeben studiert zu haben scheint," etc. He offers no proof. If one wished to make out a case for Loeben, it could bo done with his narrative poem "Ferdusi" (1817) and Heine's "Der Dichter Ferdusi." Both tell about the same story; but each tells a story that was familiar in romantic circles.

[73] In reply to a letter addressed to Professor Elster on October 4, 1914, the writer received the following most kind reply on November 23: "Die Frage, die Sie an mich richten ist leicht beantwortet: Heine hat Loeben in seinen Schriften nicht erwAehnt, aber das besagt nicht viel; er hat manchen benutzt, den er nicht nennt. Und es kann *gar keinem Zweifel unterliegen*, dass Loeben fUer die Lorelei Heines *unmittelbares* Vorbild ist;

32

Graf von Loeben and the Legend

darauf habe ich Oefter hingewiesen, aber wohl auch andere. Das Taschenbuch *Urania* fUer das Jahr 1821, wo Loebens Gedicht u. Novelle zuerst erschienen, ist unserem Dichter zweifellos zu Gesicht gekommen." No one can view Professor Elster in any other light than as an eminent authority on Heine, but his certainty here must be accepted with reserve, and his "wohl auch andere" is, in view of the fact that, he was by no means the first, and certainly not the last, to make this assertion, a trifle disconcerting.

[74] The ultimate determining of sources is an ungrateful theme. Some excellent suggestions on this subject are offered by Hans Rohl in his *Die Aeltere Romantik und die Kunst des jungen Goethe*, Berlin, 1909, pp. 70–72. This work was written under the general leadership of Professor Elster. The disciple would, in this case, hardly agree with the master. Pissin likewise speaks wisely in discussing the influence of Novalis on Loeben in his monograph on the latter, pp. 97–98. and 129–30. And Heine himself (Elster edition, V. 294) says in regard to the question whether Hegel did borrow so much from Schelling: "Nichts ist lAecherlicher als das reklamierte Eigentumsrecht an Ideen." He then shows how the ideas were not original with Schelling either; he had them from Spinoza. And it is just so here. Brentano started the legend; Heine goes back to him indirectly. Eichenidorff and Vogt directly; Schreiber borrowed from Vogt, Loeben from Schreiber, and Heine from Schreiber—and thereafter it would be impossible to say who borrowed from whom.

[75] The majority of the *Loreleidichtungen* can be found in: *Opern–Handbuch*, by Hugo Riemann, Leipzig, 1886: *Zur Geschichte der MAerchenoper*, by Leopold Schmidt, Halle, 1895; *Die Loreleysage in Dichtung und Musik*, by Hermann Seeliger, Leipzig, 1898. Seeliger took the majority of his titles from *Nassau in seinen Sagen, Geschichten und Liedern*, by Henniger, Wiesbaden, 1845. At least he says so, but one is inclined to doubt the statement, for "die meisten Balladen" have

Graf von Loeben and the Legend

been written since 1845. Seeliger's book is on the whole unsatisfactory. He has, for example, Schreiber improving on, and remodeling Loeben's saga; but Schreiber was twenty-three years older than Loeben, and wrote his saga at least three years before Loeben wrote his.

[76] In F. GrAeter's *Idunna und Hermode, eine Alterthumszeitung*, Breslau, 1812, pp. 191-92, GrAeter gives under the heading, "Die Bildergallerie des Rheins." thirty well-known German sagas. The twenty-seventh is "Der Lureley: Ein GegenstUeck zu der Fabel von der Echo." It is the version of Vogt.

[77] Aside from the above, some of the less important authors of lyrics, ballads, dramas, novels, etc., on the Lorelei-theme are: J. Bartholdi, H. Bender, H. Berg, J. P. Berger, A. H. Bernard, G. Conrad, C. Doll, L. Elchrodt, O. Fiebach, Fr. FOerster, W. Fournier, G. Freudenberg, W. Freudenberg, W. Genth, K. Geib, H. Grieben, H. GrUeneberg, G. Gurski, Henriette Heinze-Berg, A. Henniger, H. Hersch, Mary Koch, Wilhelmine Lorenz, I. Mappes, W. Molitor, Fr. MUecke, O. W. Notzsch, Luise Otto, E. RUeffer, Max Schaffroth, Luise Frelin von Sell, E. A. W. Siboni, H. Steinheuer, Adelheid von Stolterfoth, A. Storm, W. von WaldbrUehl, L. Werft, and others even more obscure than these.

[78] In Menco Stern's *Geschichten vom Rhein*, the story is told so as to connect the legend of the Lorelei with the treasures of the *Nibelungenlied*. In this way we have gold in the mountain, wine around it, a beautiful woman on it—what more could mortal wish? Sympathy! And this the Lorelei gives him in the echo. In reply to an inquiry, Mr. Stern very kindly wrote as follows: "The facts given in my *Geschichten vom Rhein* are all well known to German students; and especially those mentioned in my chapter 'Lorelay' can bo verified in the book: *Der Rhein* von Philipp F. W. Oertel (W. O. v. Horn) who was, I think, the greatest authority on the subject of the Rhine." Oertel is not an authority. In Eduard-Prokosch's *German for*

Graf von Loeben and the Legend

Beginners, the version of Schreiber was used, as is evident from the lines spoken by the Lorelei to her Father:

Vater, Vater, geschwind, geschwind. Die weissen Rosse schick' deinem Kind, Es will reiten auf Wogen und Wind.

These verses are worked into a large number of the ballads, and since they are Schreiber's own material, his saga must have had great general influence.

[79] There would be no point in listing all of the books on the legends of the Rhine that treat the story of the Lorelei. Three, however, are important, since it is interesting to see how their compilers were not satisfied with one version of the story, but included, as becomes evident on reading them, the versions of Brentano, Schreiber, Loeben, and Heine: *Der Rhein: Geschichten und Sagen*, by W. O. von Horn, Stuttgart, 1866, pp. 207–11; *Legends of the Rhine*, by H. A. Guerber, New York, 1907, pp: 199–206; *Eine Sammlung von Rhein–Sagen*, by A. Hermann Bernard, Wiesbaden, no year, pp. 225–37.

[80] Mrs. Caroline M. Sawyer wrote a poem entitled "The Lady of Lorlei. A Legend of the Rhine." It is published in *The female Poets of America*, by Rufus Wilmot Griswold, New York, 1873, p. 221. This is not the first edition of this work, nor is it the original edition of Mrs. Sawyer's ballad. It is an excellent poem. Fr. Hoebel set it to music, and Adolf Strodtmann translated it into German, because of its excellence, and included it in his *Amerikanische Anthologie*. It was impossible to determine just when Mrs. Sawyer wrote her poem. The writer is deeply indebted to Professor W. B. Cairns, of the department of English in the University of Wisconsin, who located the poem for him.

[81] Cf. *Otto Ludwigs gesammelte Schriften*, edited by Adolf Stern, Leipzig, 1801, I. 69, 107, 114.

Graf von Loeben and the Legend

[82] It has been impossible to determine just when Sucher (1789–1860) set Heine's ballad to music, but since he was professor of music at the University of TUebingen from 1817 on, and since he became interested in music while quite young, it is safe to assume that he wrote his music for "Die Lorelei" soon after its publication. The question is of some importance by way of finding out just when the ballad began to be popular. Strangely enough, there is nothing on Silcher in Hobert Eitner's compendious *Quellen-Lexicon der Musiker und Musikgelehrten der christlichen Zeitrechnung*, Leipzig, 1900–1904. Heine's ballad is included in the *Allgemeines deutsches Commersbuch unter musikalischer Redaktion von Fr. Silcher und Fr. Erck*, Strassburg, 1858 (17th ed.), but the date of composition is not given.

[83] In *Pauls Grundriss der germanischen Philologie*, I, 1039, Mogk says: "Die Weiblichen Nixen bezaubern durch ihren Gesang, die Loreley und Aehnliche Sagen mOegen hierin ihre Wurzel haben." The only trouble is, no one has thus far unearthed this saga.

[84] Wilhelm Hertz gives (pp.229–30) instances of this so that uncertainty as to its accuracy is removed. The passages are striking in that they concern the "Lorberg" and the "Lorleberg."

[85] In chap, XV Eichendorff introduces the ballad as follows: "Leontin, der wenig darauf achtgab, begann folgendes Lied Ueber ein am Rheine bekanntes MAerchen." The reference can be only to Brentano, despite the fact that the first two lines are so strongly reminiscent of Goethe's "Erlkonig." Eichendorff and Brentano became acquainted in Heidelberg and then in Berlin they were intimate. There is every reason to believe that Eichendorff knew Bretano's "RheinmAerchen" in manuscript form. For the relation of the two, see the Kosch edition of Eichendorff's works. *Briefe* and *TagebUecher,* Vols. XI–XIII.

[86] Niklas Vogt included, to be sure, in his *Jugendphantasien Ueher die Sagen des Rheins* (*ca.* 1811) an amplified

recapitulation in prose of Brentano's ballad. Schreiber knew this work, for in his *Handbuch* there is a bibliography of no fewer than ten pages of "Schriften, welche auf die Rheingegend Bezug haben." So far as one can determine such a matter from mere titles, the only one of these that could have helped him in the composition of his Lorelei–saga is: *Rheinische Geschichten und Sagen*, von Niklas Vogt. Frankfurt am Main, 1817, 6 BAende.

[87] Eduard Thorn says (p. 89): "Man darf annehmen, dass Heine die Ballade Brentano's kennen gelernt hat, dass er aus ihr den Namen entlehnte, wobei ihm Eichendorff die Fassung 'Lorelei' lieferte, und das ihm erst Loebens Auffassung der Sage zur Gestaltung verhelfen hat." It sounds like a case of *ceterum censeo*, but Thorn's argument as to Brentano and Heine is so thin that this statement too can be looked upon only as a weakly supported hypothesis.

[88] Cf. Raimund Pissin's monograph, pp. 73–74.

[89] There are about two thousand words in Schreiber's saga, and about five thousand in Loeben's.

[90] It must be remembered that Schreiber's manuals are written in an attractive style: his purpose was not simply to instruct, but to entertain. And it was not simply the legends of the Rhine and its tributaries, but those of the whole of Western Germany that he wrote up with this end in view.

[91] Some minor details that Loeben, or Heine, had he known the *MAerchen* in 1823, could have used are pointed out in Wilhelm Hertz's article, pp. 220–21.

[92] Cf. GOerres' edition, pp. 94–108.

[93] Cf. *ibid.*, pp. 128–40, and 228–44. It is in this *MAerchen* (p. 231) that Herzeleid sings Goethe's "Wer nie

sein Brod in ThrAenon asz."

[94] Cf. GOerres' edition, pp. 247–57. There are a number of details in this *MAerchen* that remind strongly of Fouque's *Undine*, which Brentano knew.

[95] In his *Die MAerchen Clemens Brentanos*, KOeln, 1895, H. Cardauns gives an admirable study of Brentano's *MAerchen*, covering the entire ground concerning the question whether Brentano's ballad was original and pointing out the sources and the value of his, *RheinmAerchen*. Cardauns comes to the only conclusion that can be reached: Brentano located his ballad in a region replete with legends, but there is no positive evidence that he did not wholly invent his own ballad. The story that Hermann Bender tells about having found an old MS dating back to the year 1650 and containing the essentials of Brentano's ballad collapses, for this MS cannot be produced, not even by Bender who claims to have found it. See Cardauns, pp. 60–67. Reinhold Steig reviewed Cardauns' book in *Euphorion* (1896, pp. 791–99) without taking in the question as to the originality of Brentano's ballad.

[96] P. 224.

[97] In Geibel's *Gesammelte Werke*, VI. 106–74, Geibel wrote the libretto for Felix Mendelssohn in 1846. Mendelssohn died before finishing it; Max Bruch completed the opera independently in 1863. It has also been set to music by two obscure composers. Karl Goedeke gives a very unsatisfactory discussion of the matter in *Emanuel Geibel*, Stuttgart, 1860. pp. 307 ff.

[98] Hermann Seeliger says (p. 73): "Zu den Bearbeitungen, die sich an die Ballade von Brentano anlehnen, gehOeren die Dichtungen von Geibel, Mohr, Roquette, Hillemacher, Fiebach und Sommer." Seeliger wrote his study for musicians, and his statement may be correct.

Graf von Loeben and the Legend

[99] Aside from the treatises on the Lorelei already mentioned, there are the following: *Zu Heines Balladen und Romanzen*, by Oskar Netoliczka, Kronstadt, 1891; this study does not treat the Lorelei; *Die Lurleisage*, by F. Rehorn, Frankfurt am Main, 1891; *Sagen und Geschichten des Rheinlandes*, by Karl Geib, Mannheim, 1836; the work is naturally long since superseded; *KOelnische Zeitung* of July 12, 1867, by H. Grieben; *KOelnische Zeitung* of 1855, by H. DUentzer; *H. Heine, ein Vortrag*, by H. Sintenis, pp. 21–26; *Die Lorelei: Die Loreleidichtungen mit besonderer RUecksicht auf die Ballade von Heinr. Heine*, by C. L. Leimbach, WolfenbUettel, 1879. The last six of these works were not accessible, but, since they are quoted by the accessible studies, it seems that they offer nothing new. (The writer has since secured Leimbach's treatise of 50 small pages. It offers nothing new.)

[100] Adolf Seybert in his *Die Loreleisage*, Wiesbaden, 1863 and 1872 (Programm), contends that Frau Holla and the Lorelei are related. Fritz Strich in his *Die Mythologie in der deutschen Literatur von Klopstock bis Wagner*, Halle, 1910, says (pp. 307–9) that Brentano's ballad is "eine mythologische Erfindung Brentanos, zu der ihn der echoreiche Felsen dieses Namens bei Bacharach anregte." He also says: "Ob nicht Heines Lied auf Brentanos Phantasie zurUeckgewirkt haben mag?" The reference is to Brentano's *MAerchen*. Strich's book contains a detailed account of the use of mythology in Heine, Loeben, and Brentano.

[101] Hermann Seeliger says (p. 8): "Ich meine, die ganze romantische Schule hAette ohne den Stoff vom Volke zu bekommen, ein Gedicht von solcher SchOenheit wie das von Brentano weder gemacht noch machen kOennen." Vis–a–vis such a statement, sociability ceases.

CPSIA information can be obtained at www.ICGtesting.com
Printed in the USA
BVOW04*1712060715

407337BV00013B/25/P